T0196627

Make Taxes Great Again

The Good, The Bad And The Ugly About Tax Reform

Patrice Tudor, EA

authorHOUSE®

AuthorHouse™
1663 Liberty Drive
Bloomington, IN 47403
www.authorhouse.com
Phone: 1 (800) 839-8640

Published by AuthorHouse   12/06/2018

ISBN: 978-1-5462-7096-6 (sc)
ISBN: 978-1-5462-7095-9 (e)

Library of Congress Control Number: 2018914278

Print information available on the last page.

Any people depicted in stock imagery provided by Getty Images are models, and such images are being used for illustrative purposes only. Certain stock imagery © Getty Images.

This book is printed on acid-free paper.

Because of the dynamic nature of the Internet, any web addresses or links contained in this book may have changed since publication and may no longer be valid. The views expressed in this work are solely those of the author and do not necessarily reflect the views of the publisher, and the publisher hereby disclaims any responsibility for them.

Table of Content

Dedication

This book is dedicated to three very
amazing women in my life.

Patricia Brown, Nyla Ward and Sonia Booker

Introduction

What Is The Tax Cuts & Jobs Act and What You Should Know

On December 20, 2017, Congress passed the largest tax reform legislation in more than three decades ago, actually since 1986. The House approved H.R. 1, now known as the "Tax Cuts and Jobs Act," or "TCJA". This sweeping tax reform was passed, by a vote of 224 to 201. The new tax reform which was signed into law On December 22, 2017 by President Donald Trump brings sweeping changes to how Americans report and pay taxes. The new tax reform makes monumental changes in the tax laws for both individuals and businesses. Many of the individual tax provisions in the Tax Cuts and Jobs Act are only temporary with no guarantee that a future Congress will extend them. The changes for individual taxpayers took effect in 2018 and are scheduled to "sunset" after 2025. Conversely, most of the business provisions in the new law are permanent.

Most of the provisions kicked in on January 1, 2018 and therefore they didn't affect 2017 tax filings but will greatly impact the 2018 tax season. Much of the tax reform applies to tax years beginning before Jan. 1, 2026. In order to meet budget, most of the changes contain a "sunset," or an expiration date and are temporary for over 5 years so that it can comply with certain budgetary constraints. Which means that in 5 years tax legislation could have another drastic change and revert to former legislation or remain the same

Based on my most current analysis of the tax reform and from an abstract point of view the summary of the research concludes that the "winners" of the tax reform are Entrepreneurs (self-employed), Business Owners, Corporations and Real estate investors. And do you know Why? Because the single most important worldwide strategy if you want to obtain and retain wealth is to engage in legal tax strategies that educate and implement tax laws that reduce your tax liability and thereby allowing you to pay less taxes. Unlike in the past, because of the new tax reform the United States is NOW a tax haven for other countries.

Taxes ARE complicated however the original forethought of the tax reform was to help simplify taxes. Believe it or not, although at the time of this writing we are only a few weeks away from the upcoming tax season there is still a huge mystery surrounding these changes and certain aspects of the reform is still at various stages in the legislative process. The tax plan is only a framework, with many details yet to be filled in. Even as a highly trained tax professional that has completed over 100+ hours of continuing education on TCJA, I still find myself learning new information daily whether I am visiting the IRS website, attending conferences or talking to my colleagues. I wanted to take my extensive research on the topic and break it down in a way that would be easy to understand.

Chapter 1

The Good, The Bad and The Ugly – What Does TCJA Mean For You and Your Family

The Tax Cuts and Jobs Act (TCJA) will involve the taxes of almost all taxpayers and with all the buzz about tax reform many taxpayers are questioning how this change will affect **THEIR** tax return. Each person, taxpayer, household and business has their own unique "tax story" and a tax return is as unique as a fingerprint.....no two tax returns are alike. So, although the Good, the Bad and the Ugly of the tax reform is in the eye of the beholder (subjective). There may be aspects that are viewed as "good" by some and "bad" by others or may not even apply to you, your family or your business.

Most taxpayers will be wondering about what is in the bill and how it might affect them and trust me when I tell you that nearly every taxpayer **WILL** be impacted. The content in this book is intended for educational purposes ONLY and is NOT tax advice. When comes to tax matters it is always best to seek the counsel of a trusted, well vetted and highly credentialed tax professional. This book is written to be informative, unbiased, non-partisan and neutral regarding tax reform and will point out some resources that may help you better understand the legislation, address the chief tax provisions AND the most notable changes that will most likely affect you, your family and businesses, including valuable information about the increase in the standard deduction, changes to itemized deductions, suspension of personal exemptions, changes to the Child Tax Credit (CTC) and other family-based credits….just to name a few. The changes discussed here are just the tip of a massive "tax" iceberg.

Chapter 2

The Good – You and Your family

Let's begin by looking at some of the "Good" changes and tax relief for individuals and families. These are changes that are viewed as favorable because they could result in you having a larger refund (and who wouldn't want that 😊) or having a reduction your tax liability. Lower tax rates and higher tax brackets mean the amount of taxable income would generally result in a lower effective tax rate. Let's check out some of the "Good" changes below:

Income Tax Rates & Brackets - (NEW)

Tax rate schedules for people are based on their filing status—i.e., married, single, married filing jointly, married filing separately, head of household—each of which is divided into ranges of income that are taxed at gradually higher marginal tax rates as income surges. Under the pre-Act law, individuals were subject to tax rates: 10%, 15%, 25%, 28%, 33%, 35%, and 39.6%.

Under the Tax Cuts & Jobs Act (TCJA), tax brackets for individuals are as follows: 10%, 12%, 22%, 24%, 32%, 35%, and 37%. The tax brackets for estates and trusts are as follows: 10%, 24%, 35%, and 37%. This benefits mainly middle income and high-income taxpayers.

Pre-Reform	Rate	Tax Cuts & Jobs Act	Rate
$0 -$9,325 Individual $0 - $18,650 Joint	10%	0- $9,525 Individual 0 - $19,500 Joint	10%
$9,325 - $37,950 Individual $18,650-75,900 Joint	15%	$9,526 - $38,700 Individual $19,500-$77,400 Joint	12%
$37,950 - $91,900 Individual $75,900 -$153,100 Joint	25%	$38,701 - $82,500 Individual $77,401-$165,000 Joint	22%
$91,900 - $191,650 Individual $153,100-$233,350 Joint	28%	$82,500 - $157,500 Individual $165,001-$315,000 Joint	24%
$191,650 - $416,700 Individual $233,350-$416,700 Joint	33%	$157,500 - $200,000 Individual $315,001-$400,000 Joint	32%
$416,700 - $418,400 Individual $416,700 - $470,700 Joint	35%	$200,001 - $500,000 Individual $400,001 -$600,000	35%
Over $418,400 Individual Over $470,700 Joint	39.6%	Over $500,000 Individual Over $600,0001	37%

Standard Deduction - Increased

The standard deduction is the fixed dollar amount that the IRS allows you to deduct if you choose not to itemize your deductions and it reduces your taxable federal income. The new tax law increases the standard deduction. The standard deduction will nearly double on your 2018 tax year return. Taxpayers that have the filing status of "single" will see their standard deductions jump from $6,350 in 2017 to $12,000 for the 2018 tax year. Married couples who file jointly, will see an increase from $12,700 to $24,000. You may be asking, "Why is this so important"??? Well, it's because the standard deduction and itemized deductions reduce the taxpayers adjusted gross income (AGI) which in turn helps to determine their taxable income. The lower the taxable income…The lower the tax liability!!! Approximately 30% of all taxpayers itemize and as a result of the increased standard deduction fewer households will itemize. Under this new law, the percentage of people that itemize is likely to fall. The new law also eliminates the so-called "marriage penalty" by removing many of the disadvantages of the married filing separately filing status. The new law eliminates the discrepancy in income thresholds between a head of household filer and a single individual for all income subject to the 24% rate and above.

Child Tax Credit - Increased

Before TCJA, taxpayers could claim a child tax credit of up to $1,000 per qualifying child under the age of 17. The Child Tax Credit increased from $1,000 per child up to $2,000. Additionally, the amount that is refundable increased from $1,100 up to $1,400 per qualifying child. So, you may be asking yourself what's a "refundable" credit. Refundable credits have a dual tax function. First, they can reduce the amount of tax you owe AND secondly, if you qualify for the refundable portion of the credit and if the amount of the credit is larger than the taxes you owe, you will be eligible to receive the difference and this "extra" credit will be refunded to you.

Yay…more money in your pockets!!! Additionally, the new Adjusted Gross Income (AGI) phase-out thresholds increased from $110,000 to $400,000 for taxpayers who were married, filing jointly and $200,000 for all other taxpayers which means more taxpayers can qualify for the credit and will be eligible to receive more of the credit than in the past including high income earners who previously did not qualify for the credit due to the income phase-out-threshold.

Non-Dependent Tax Credit - (NEW)

The bill added a new, non-refundable credit of $500 for dependents other than your children and those that do not qualify for the child tax credit including elderly and disabled dependents such as parents. The credit is for certain non-child-based dependents such as relatives that are aged 18 or over who live with you. The IRS defines a qualifying relative in Section 152(a) as 1) an individual who bears a specific relationship to the taxpayer 2) whose gross income for the calendar year is less than the exemption amount 3) who receives over one-half of their support from the taxpayer and is 4) not a qualifying child of the taxpayer or any other taxpayer. So, the 'usual' rules for claiming a non-child dependent include that you must provide over 50% of their support, they must have less than $4050 of income, and they either need to be closely related to your or live with you the entire year. This is a great benefit for those individuals and families that are caring for members of their household that may or may not be closely related by blood or marriage but are being supported by them.

Health Care Mandate - Repealed

This topic has received a lot of media attention and under the new tax reform, there's the repeal of the Affordable Care Act (ACA) individual mandate. This removes the tax penalty for those that don't have health insurance AFTER December 31, 2018. So now those taxpayers that are not insured are no longer subject to having the penalty accessed on their tax return. The individual shared responsibility payment is now reduced to ZERO. This is great news for taxpayers that have been unable to obtain or afford healthcare insurance.

Medical Expenses – Threshold lowered

Under the TCJA, it lowers the threshold in which unreimbursed medical expenses can be deducted. So, for 2017 and the 2018 medical expenses, you can subtract medical expenses which are larger than 7.5% of your accustomed gross revenue contrast to the greater 10%.

Sec 529 Education Plan - Expanded

The Sec 529 plan is a tax-advantaged savings plan designed to encourage people to save for future education costs. Before tax reform, individuals that participated in a Sec 529 Plan could only use the distributions to pay for qualified college education expenses. A Sec 529 plan account would allow non-deductible contributions and provide for tax-free growth if distributions were used for post-secondary education expenses. Eligible schools include colleges, universities, vocational schools, or other postsecondary schools that participate in federal student aid programs by the Department of Education.

However, now under the new law, people have permission to use Section 529 accounts to save for certain elementary and secondary education expenses AND for higher education. The plan's scope was increased beyond higher education to allow tax-free distributions of up to $10,000 per year for grammar and high school education tuition and expenses. For distributions after December 31, 2017, "qualified higher education expenses" include tuition at public elementary and secondary schools, private, or religious school and includes tuition, fees, books, supplies, reasonable room and board if the student was enrolled at least half-time and required equipment. You may be able to deduct qualified education expenses paid during the year for yourself, your spouse and your qualified dependents. The caveat is that you cannot claim the Sec 529 deduction if your filing status is married filing separately or if another person can claim you as a dependent their tax return. This is an awesomely good change for those that had been limited to using the plan only for their college age dependents. Now families can utilize this to cover the entire duration of their dependent (s) education expenses, literally from kindergarten to college. This will help incentivize the Sec 529 plan for families.

Student Loan Forgiveness - Relief

Starting in 2018, forgiveness of student loan debt will not be taxable income to the student because of the student's death or total disability. This change provides relief for those taxpayers that have had the misfortune of death or disability. Many people don't know and are quite surprised when they must include cancelled student loan debt as income on their tax return. They seem to find it unfair and a bit daunting but now this will no longer be the case.

Tuition & Fee Deduction - Extended

Tuition and Fees Deduction has been extended and made available through 2017 as part of the Bipartisan Budget Act of 2018. The tuition and fees deduction is an above-the-line deduction which means you can claim this deduction even if you don't itemize. This can be beneficial to you and your family even if you didn't qualify for the American Opportunity Tax Credit (AOTC) or the Lifetime Learning Credit because you may still be able to claim the tuition and education related expenses on your tax return. This deduction had expired at the end of 2016 but because the Bipartisan Budget Act was signed into law by President Trump on February 9, 2018, the tuition and fees deduction was renewed. If have already filed your 2017 return and find out that you are eligible to claim this credit then this is great news because you can now file an amended return on Form 1040X and claim the credit. It is unknown if it will be extended through other legislation for 2018 so take advantage of this extension (if you qualify) as soon as possible.

Charitable Contribution Deduction Limitation - Increased

In the past, an individual's charitable contribution was limited by the IRS and would only allow charitable contributions that generally did not exceed 50% of a taxpayer's adjusted gross income (AGI). The applicable percentages were 50%, 30%, or 20% depending on the type of organization and there was a 50% limitation applied to public charities and certain private foundations.

Under the TCJA, the tax-deductible contribution allowable amounts that are made after Dec. 31, 2017 but before Jan. 1, 2026, have increased from 50% to 60% for cash contributions to public charities and certain private foundations. Contributions exceeding the 60% limitation are generally allowed to be carried forward and deducted for up to five years. This is really good especially since several of the other typical itemized deductions have been eliminated. (I will discuss more about the disappearing deductions in the next chapter)

Estate and Gift Tax

There was an effort to get rid of the federal estate tax however the efforts to kill the federal estate tax fell short. The new law doubles the amount from 5 million to 10 million that can be left to heirs tax-free in 2018. The tax-free amount goes to about $11 million for singles and about $22 million for married couples. The amount is scheduled to rise each year in order to keep up with inflation. This enhanced exclusion applies to estates of decedents dying, generation skipping transfers made, and gifts made after 2017, but is scheduled to sunset after December 31, 2025.

Chapter 3

The Bad– You and Your family

So now for "The Bad"! 🙁 There were several changes made that either eliminated or reduced some of the most beloved deductions. This could possibly lead to increased tax liability for taxpayers who generally rely heavily on these types of deductions. Itemized deductions such as home mortgage interest, local and state income taxes, property taxes and sales taxes were either reduced, capped or totally eliminated. Let's check out a few of the more prevalent deductions that were either reduced or eliminated.

Personal and Dependent Exemptions – Eliminated

The bill eliminates the personal and dependent exemptions which are currently $4,050 for 2017 and was expected to increase to $4,150 in 2018. Taxpayers will no longer have the benefit of reducing their taxable income based on the number of exemptions they have.

State and Local Tax Deduction (SALT) - Limited

Pre-reform, taxpayers could deduct several types of taxes paid at the local and state level, including real taxes, personal property taxes, income taxes, and sales taxes from their taxable income as an itemized deduction. Starting on January 1, 2018, the bill limited the amount of local taxes, state property taxes, income taxes, and sales taxes that can be deducted. These taxes are now limited to $10,000 ($5,000 for a married taxpayer filing a separate return). The new law set a maximum limit of how much you can write off, generally these taxes have been fully tax deductible. This could be extremely unpleasant for taxpayers that live in areas that have high tax rates and costly property taxes. Homeowners in states such as California and New York, which both have extremely high property taxes, will feel the effects of this change. By the way, when taxpayers heard about the upcoming SALT limitation, a lot of them rushed to prepay future year taxes in tax year 2017 in hopes of maximizing on the deduction before the limitation kicked in. Well to their surprise, the TCJA prohibited taxpayers from being able to actually claim prepayment of future taxes on their 2017 tax return. What a bummer ☹ This was a huge disappointment.

Mortgage Interest Deduction – Capped/Limited

Prior to the new reform, taxpayers could deduct the interest paid on qualified mortgage loans as an itemized deduction. This included interest that was paid on a mortgage which is then secured by a second residence or a principal residence. Lawmakers decided to reduce the amount of debt on which homeowners can deduct mortgage interest from $1 million to $750,000. In the old law, the mortgage interest was capped at $1 million. The new law lowers it to $750,000 but this does not apply to existing mortgages. Older loans are still subject to the $1 million cap. The bad news is it applies to all new mortgages. The new limit applies to mortgage debt and loans incurred on or before December 15, 2017 and binding contracts before December 15, 2017

Interest Deduction on Home Equity Loans - Eliminated

The new law ends the home-equity debt deduction IMMEDIATELY. The law repeals the deduction of interest accrued on home-equity debt after December 31, 2017. This applies to both old home equity loans and new home-equity debt if the money is used for any purpose other than to buy, build or improve a principal or second home. Additionally, there's no "grandfather" clause to help people with existing lines of credit and this is scheduled to stay in effect until 2025.

Chapter 4

The Ugly – You and Your Family

What's "The Ugly"???? Well, with the new reform there were deductions that were placed in limbo. This leaves taxpayers guessing as to when and if these deductions will ever become available again. They were neither reduced or eliminated but merely just suspended for unknown reasons. With the suspension, these deductions may be reinstated after 2025 but the ugly part about this is that we don't know what will happen. The following suspended deductions can play a pivotal role on a tax return and the fact that they will not be available for taxpayers should be a cause of great concern.

Alimony Deduction by Payor/Inclusion by Payee – Suspended

Alimony payment use allow the payer of the alimony to claim an above-the-line deduction for qualified payments and the recipient would then have to report this as income on their return. This typically was a great way for the payer to reduce the volume of income they had to pay taxes on. BUT not anymore! Now, both divorce and separation agreements executed after December 31, 2018 will no longer allow alimony or separation maintenance payments to be tax deductible by the payer and the recipient will not be required to include the payments as income on their tax return. This new law also applies to existing agreements modified after December 31, 2018. The effective date of this provision is delayed by one year and unlike many of the provisions affecting individuals that are subject to sunset after 2025, the alimony changes are not scheduled to expire.

Miscellaneous Itemized Deduction– Suspended

Beginning after December 31, 2017 and before January 1, 2026, all miscellaneous itemized deductions subject to the 2% of AGI limit threshold are suspended. This Includes deductions for unreimbursed employee business expenses, tax preparation fees, money spent on job training, investment expenses, hobby expenses and certain casualty losses. Prior to the new tax reform, taxpayers could deduct certain miscellaneous itemized deductions if those expenses exceeded, 2% of the taxpayer's adjusted gross income (AGI). Although, the miscellaneous itemized deduction 2% limit criteria was pretty tough for most filers to reach, it was not impossible and will be missed by those that could take advantage of this tax break.

Moving Deduction & Reimbursements– Suspended

When I found out that the Moving Deduction was suspended, I instantly thought of all the millennials, recent college grads and those embarking on new careers that are relocating and entering a new chapter of their lives. I remember moving from NC to Tx after graduating college and I was so relieved when

I found out that at least a portion of the thousands of dollars I spent relocating would be able to provide a little bit of tax relief when I filled my return especially since I was now making more money and being faced with potential tax bill....yikes. Deduction for the expenses of moving is now suspended, except for active duty members of the Armed Forces and their families that have a military ordered move. The moving deduction is suspended up until 2025.

For the tax years that are prior to 2018 (pre-tax reform), the **IRS** allowed taxpayers to deduct **eligible** job-related moving expenses from their taxable income they report on Form 1040. This deduction was not subject to any limits, so you could claim all your **qualified moving** costs if you meet the 3 eligibility requirements. If your move passed the 3-requirement test of 1) Move Related test: Move must be related to the start of work. 2) Distance test: Your new work place was at least 50 miles from your old home/old work place 3) Time test: Must work full-time for at least 39 weeks during the first 12 months immediately following your arrival, for more information see Publication 521, *Moving Expenses*

Suspension of the deduction for moving expenses can be expected to increase the cost of relocating employees. Businesses required to move employees to meet their business needs could face significantly higher costs after considering the gross-up for taxes.

Deduction for Personal Casualty & Theft Losses – Suspended (unless declared a federal disaster)

Before the TCJA, taxpayers were generally allowed to claim an itemized deduction for non-reimbursed personal casualty losses, including those arising from fire, storm, other casualty, or from theft.

Under the new law, for tax years beginning after Dec. 31, 2017 and before January 1, 2026, the personal casualty and theft loss deduction is suspended, EXCEPT for personal casualty losses incurred in a disaster declared by the President under Sec 401 of the Robert T Stafford Disaster Relief and Emergency Assistance Act (Federally-declared disaster). (https://tax.thomsonreuters.com/news/2017-tax-reform-checkpoint-special-study-on-individual-tax-changes-in-the-tax-cuts-and-jobs-act/, n.d.)

Chapter 5

No Change – You and Your Family

There were several familiar tax laws that were not subject to any reform and I thought they deserved an honorable mention since 1 out of every 3 taxpayers will be have at least one of these on their tax return.

Earned Income Tax Credit (also known as EIC or EITC)

Let's start with one of the fan favorites…. Earned Income Credit also more commonly known as EIC. Earned Income Tax Credit (EITC) is a refundable credit for taxpayers that have low to moderate incomes. In all my years as a tax professional this is one of the most popular and most talked about tax credits and I am glad that it was retained because so many working taxpayers and their families rely on this refundable credit every year. This credit is meant to supplement your EARNED income. Earned income can be your wages, salary or business income you earn if you are self-employed. If you qualify for the Earned Income Tax Credit you can reduce your taxes and increase your tax refund. The EITC allows working people and their families to keep more of their hard-earned money.

Student Loan Interest Deduction

Are you one of the more than 1.3 million students that graduated with student loan debt? Well, if you are then you will be relieved to know that the student loan interest deduction was retained and was not subject to any changes. Generally, personal interest you pay is not deductible on your tax return with the exception certain mortgage interest. However, there is a special deduction allowed for the interest that has been paid during the tax year on qualified student loan payments. If your modified adjusted gross income (MAGI) is less than $80,000 ($160,000 if filing a joint return), there's typically a deduction allowed for interest on the repayment of loans that were obtained and used for higher education while you or your spouse were students. This deduction applies for both mandatory repayment or voluntary payments made on qualified student loans. This deduction can reduce the amount of your income subject to tax by up to $2,500. (Tax Benefits for Education: Information Center, n.d.)

The student loan interest deduction, just like the Tuition and Fees deduction is an "above-the-line deduction" and therefore is taken as an adjustment to income, which means you can claim this deduction even if you do not itemize deductions on Form 1040's Schedule A.

American Opportunity Credit (AOTC)

The American Opportunity Credit (AOTC) is a post-secondary education tax credit of up to $2,500 per year, per student for up to four years. Up to 40% of the credit is refundable and has a phase-out threshold of $160,000 if your filing status is

Married Filing Joint (MFJ) status and $80,000 for others. However, there is no credit allowed if your filing status is Married Filing Separate (MFS).

Lifetime Learning Credit (LLC)

The Lifetime Learning Credit (LLC), remained the same, and it provides an annual credit of up to $2,000 per family for post-secondary education. The credit has a phase-out threshold of $112,000 for Married Filing Joint (MFJ) filers, $56,000 for others and no credit allowed for those Married Filing Separate (MFS) taxpayers.

Coverdell Education Accounts

Unlike the Sec 529 plan, (which had a major change) the laws governing the Coverdell Education account didn't change at all. The Coverdell Educations accounts are not tax deductible but the annual contribution of up to $2,000 can grow tax free if the distributions are used for grammar school and qualified education expenses.

Home Sale Tax Exclusion

The Home Sale Tax Exclusion still allows taxpayers to exclude gains of up to $500,000 for MFJ and $250,000 for all others if they own and use the home as their principal and primary residence for at least 2 out of the 5 years prior to its sale.

Educator Expenses Deduction

Continues to allow up to $250 for classroom supplies and professional development courses.

Performing Artists Expenses

An above-the-line deduction for performing arts employees that have expenses that exceed 10% of their AGI however they must have an AGI of $16,000 or less.

Dependent Care Assistance - Exclusion from gross income of up to $5,000 per year for employer provided dependent care assistance.

Adoption Assistance - Exclusion for qualified adoption expenses paid or reimbursed by an employer. The exclusion is phased out for higher-income taxpayers.

Gambling Losses – Continues to allow a deduction for gambling losses not to exceed the gambling income.

Exclusion for Interest on U.S. Savings Bonds used for Higher Education Expenses – Excludable interest earned on a qualified United States Series EE savings bond issued after 1989 is excludable proceeds of used to pay for higher education expenses. The exclusion is phased out for higher income taxpayers.

Chapter 6

What Does TCJA Mean For Solopreneurs, Entrepreneurs and Business

The Tax Cuts and Jobs Act has numerous changes for business. Some of the critical changes in business include lowering the corporate rate to 21%, lowering the tax liability for certain pass-through business income, increased expensing of capital items, limiting business interest deductions, modifying the NOL deduction, limiting Like-kind exchanges to only real property and the repeal of the corporate alternative minimum tax (AMT). The final tax reform bill contains several provisions affecting Solopreneurs, entrepreneurs and business. Here is a quick overview of the Good, the Bad and the Ugly for Solopreneurs, entrepreneurs and business.

Chapter 7

The Good - Solopreneurs, Entrepreneurs and Business

The Tax Cuts and Jobs Act (TCJA) provides new deductions for certain business income earned for tax years beginning in 2018, including loss limitations were expanded. These provisions are relevant to a lot of business owners conducting business as pass through entries and sole proprietorships. Although most of the corporate (business) changes are permanent certain provisions are scheduled to sunset after 2025

Corporate Tax Rate - Reduced Permanently

The new law slashes the tax rate on regular corporations. One of the biggest changes includes a reduction in the top corporate rate from 35% to 21%, effective Jan 1, 2018. TCJA permanently reduced the corporate tax rate to 21 percent. If you own a C-corporation that owns real estate, then you will enjoy the new tax cut. Corporations in America will start from 2018 paying 21% tax instead of the traditional 35%. This is an important tax cut and will effectively make sure that you save more on taxes in your C-corporation. Real estate investors and small business owners that have formed corporations can benefit and enjoy the reduction of corporate tax.

Tax Relief for Passthrough Businesses

A new 20% deduction for incomes from certain type of "pass-through" entities such as partnerships and S-Corps (C corporations do not qualify for this deduction). The law offers a different kind of relief to individuals who own entities that pass their income to their owners for tax purposes, as well as sole proprietors who report income on Schedule C of their tax returns. Starting in 2018, many of these taxpayers will be allowed to deduct 20% of their qualifying income before figuring their tax bill.

20% tax deduction for self-employed filers

If you are a solopreneur, freelancer, independent contractor, or have a gig on the side you may qualify to receive a 20% Qualified Business Income Deduction on your qualified business net income. This could save your business money because the TCJA tax reform allows deductions for qualified business income for pass-through entities. Qualified business income is the net amount of your business income, expenses and deductions for your business. Qualified business income includes:

- Business income from services and from rental real estate
- Sole proprietorships and pass-through income from partnerships, S-corporations, estates and trusts qualifies for this deduction

It must be noted that the deductions are contingent upon TCJA eligibility requirements including Section 707 of the Act. The TCJA modifies the depreciable period for real estate properties and this can affect your finances. This deduction will reduce taxable income on your federal tax return and because the overall federal income tax rates were lowered for taxpayers, you may see a further reduction in tax rates. This is because business income that passes through to someone who is self-employed or to an individual from a pass-through entity will be taxed at individual tax rates less the deduction of up to 20% to bring the tax rate lower. For a sole proprietor in the 24% bracket, for example, excluding 20% of income from taxation would have the effect of lowering the tax rate to 19.2%.

Some important details about this deduction is that the deduction may be phased out based on taxable income. The deduction is limited to 20% of the lesser of the net qualified business income or your taxable income before the deduction and after reduction for any net capital gain. If your business is considered a specified service business and the taxable income exceeds the threshold amount of $157,500 for single filers and $315,000 for joint filers, the deduction is reduced pro-rata.

The phase-in is complete when income reaches $207,500 for single filers and $415,000 for joint filers. Any income above these upper thresholds, you get no deduction. To put it simply, taxpayers who have income below the lower income threshold have no worries at all and are entitled to the full deduction. However, individuals in certain service professions that are traditionally high-paid, such as doctors and lawyers, may not qualify for any deduction. The deduction for taxpayers in other businesses can vary widely.

In the past, people who own businesses that own real estate often avoided the C-corporation because of double taxation. The good news is that all pass-through business income is not taxed under the new law. The law gives all business that passes income to the owners a 20% deduction including C-corps.

If you own a real estate entity that passes the income to you for reporting on your personal tax return then you can deduct 20% of the taxable income. This effectively brings down the income tax rate form pass-through income from a high of 37% to 29.6%. This represents huge savings especially if your income is high.

Maximum Tax on Capital Gains is Fixed at 20%

The act prescribes the maximum tax applicable for the individual capital gain tax to be 20%. Capital gain tax is usually a major factor that influences the real estate property business. The tax having been prescribed to be levied at a maximum of 20%, real estate proprietors can operate with some elevated level of certainty. Such certainty is that upon the sale or realization of real property including but not limited to the sale of land, building or a section of a building; the capital gain shall be changed at a rate not exceeding 20%.

Section 179 Business Expense Deduction - Increased

Solopreneurs, entrepreneurs and businesses will be able to benefit from an increase of the Section 179 Business Deduction. When you purchase equipment for your business you may be able to take advantage of this purchase because there is an almost doubling of the amount you can expense.

The annual expensing and investment threshold limits are increased from 510,000 to $1,000,000. For property placed in service after 2017: The Definition of Sec 179 property expanded to include certain depreciable tangible personal property –for example furniture, refrigerators, ranges and for qualified business equipment like computers and printers. TCJA has expanded the definition of qualified real property eligible for Sec 179. Section 179 now includes nonresidential real property improvements placed into service after 2017 such as roofs, heating and cooling equipment and security systems.

Depreciation Expense Deduction for Business Vehicles - Increased

One of the biggest changes brought about for business by the TCJA was in the depreciation expense for business vehicles. Now there is a huge increase allowed for business vehicle deductions. One perk for using your car for your business is that you'll see an increase in the maximum allowable depreciation expense which further reduces your taxable self-employment and business income. If you purchased a six-passenger vehicle under 14,000 pounds, you can deduct up to $25,000 in the first year you purchased the vehicle for your business if you use it at least 50% of the time for business. This change will most likely result in more business owners buying cars versus leasing.

Property and Sales Taxes on Rental Property -Retained

Unlike for individuals and families, property and sales taxes will remain deductible for taxpayers in a business or for-profit activity. For example, if you own a residential rental property, you can continue to fully deduct property taxes paid on that property.

Corporate Alternative Minimum Tax (AMT) - Repealed

The Tax Cuts and Jobs Act repealed the alternative minimum tax (AMT) on corporations. Alternative Minimum Tax (AMT) was designed to reduce high income earners and businesses ability to avoid taxes. Over the years, the AMT system has not properly been indexed for inflation, which has caused more middle-income taxpayers to be subject to AMT. Under the Tax Cuts and Jobs Act, the individual Alternative Minimum Tax (AMT) exemption and exemption phase-out was increased to properly align with the current cost-of-living. AMT is a separate method of determining tax liability and was modified in the new law to ensure it served its intended purpose. Prior to the Act, the corporate AMT tax rate was 20 percent. Under new law, the corporate AMT is repealed for the tax years beginning after Dec. 31, 2017.

The new law increases the AMT exemption and exemption phase-out. The new tax act allows corporations to offset regular tax liability by any minimum tax credit they may have for any tax year. Corporations that have been subject to AMT and have a credit carryforward will be able to use the credit to offset taxes in the next few years. All corporations should be able to use various tax benefits in full to offset taxable income without the limits imposed by the AMT. Companies that have an Alternative Minimum Tax Credit for AMT paid in prior years will be allowed to use the credit, subject to limits, in full before 2022. Furthermore, any unused minimum tax credit is refundable during the period from 2018 to 2021 based on the following tax years:

- Tax Years Beginning in 2018 – 2020: The refundable credit amount is equal to 50 percent of the excess of the minimum tax credit for the tax year, over the amount allowable for the year against regular tax liability.
- Tax Years Beginning in 2021: The refundable credit amount is equal to 100 percent of the excess of the minimum tax credit for the tax year, over the amount allowable for the year against regular tax liability. (https://doeren.com/tax-reform-individual-amt-corporate-amt/, n.d.)

So what does all this mean???? Well it translates to a lower tax liability and may even result in a refund. (cha-ching $$$$$)

Chapter 8

The Bad - Solopreneurs, Entrepreneurs and Business

Tax planning is so essential when it comes to understanding the new tax reform and how it may negatively affect your business based on the business tax laws that were recently repealed. Staying aware and informed of the changes is the best way to forge ahead in your business and make sure you remain open minded and proactive. The really "Bad" part of the reform as it relates to business is that these changes can cause HUGE unexpected and unavoidable tax burdens for solopreneurs, entrepreneurs and businesses. if they are not proactive when it comes down to the new business tax laws that were repealed monstrous tax burden could be on the horizon.

Like-Kind Exchange (Sec 1031 Exchange) - Repealed

Section 1031 Exchange (Like-kind exchange) is a non-recognition of gain when taxpayers trade properties and assets of like-kind that are used for business or investment. Before the new reform, exchanges of personal property such as art, vehicles, equipment and intellectual property rights were subject to restrictive IRS rules but were still allowed. Now with the TCJA in-place, the only asset that qualifies for Sec 1031 exchange treatment rules completed after December 31, 2017will be real property. Sec 1031 Exchange, was originally intended to encourage active reinvestment and help manage unfair taxation of investments. This use to be a great tax loophole for the trade and business. This change is damaging because like-kind exchanges were an excellent way to build tax-deferred wealth for business owners, farmers and investors.

Net Operating Loss (NOL) Deduction carryback provision - Repealed

In the past, Net Operation Losses may be carried back for 2 years on a tax return and any remaining balance is then carried forward until it is all used up or a maximum of 20 years unless the taxpayer elects to forego the carryback and carry the loss forward only.

Beginning after December 31, 2017, the NOL deduction was limited to 80% of the taxable income (determined without regard to the NOL deduction) for losses arising in taxable years beginning after December 31, 2017. The 2-year carryback provision was repealed after 2017 except for certain farm losses and what's huge is that now NOL's can be carried forward indefinitely.

Excess Business Losses for Individuals

Losses, other than passive losses, were allowed, and if a net loss was the result, a NOL deduction was created and carried back 2 years and then forward 20 years until used up. A taxpayer other than a C corporation would not be allowed an "excess business loss." Instead, the loss would be carried forward and treated as part of the taxpayer's net operating loss (NOL) carryforward in subsequent taxable years. Excess business loss for a taxable year is defined in the Act as the excess of the taxpayer's aggregate deductions attributable to the taxpayer's trades or businesses for that year, over the sum of the taxpayer's aggregate gross income or gain for the year plus a "threshold amount" of $500,000 for married individuals filing jointly, or $250,000 for other individuals. The provision will apply after taking into account the passive activity loss rules. Limitations on net operating loss (NOLs) deductions to 80 percent of taxable income for losses incurred after 2017.

Domestic Production Deduction (Sec 199) - Repealed

Sec 199 provides a deduction from taxable income (AGI in the case of an individual), equal to 9% of the lesser of the taxpayer's qualified domestic production activities income or taxable income (determined without regard to the section 199 deduction) for the taxable year. The deduction is further limited to 50% of the W-2 wages paid by the taxpayer that are allocable to domestic production gross receipts for the year.

Chapter 9

The Ugly - Solopreneurs, Entrepreneurs and Business

Well let's talk about a few of "The Ugly" parts of the change as it relates to solopreneurs, entrepreneurs and business!!! TCJA established additional limitations on the deductibility of certain business meals and entertainment expenses. These changes are going to be unpleasant and somewhat objectionable for almost everyone and every business that is affected.

Entertainment Expenses - Limited

Prior to the tax reform, a taxpayer who could establish that their entertainment expenses and meals were directly related to (or associated with) the active conduct of their trade or business, generally could deduct 50% of that expense. The deductions for entertainment expenses that are directly related to or associated with the conduct of business are now repealed.

Under the act, entertainment expenses incurred or paid after Dec. 31, 2017 are nondeductible unless they fall under the specific exceptions in Code Section 274(e). The Tax Cuts and Jobs Act now disallows deductions for activities considered to be entertainment, amusement, or recreation. Solopreneurs, entrepreneurs and business can no longer deduct membership dues for any club organized for business, pleasure, recreation, or other social purpose nor any function or facility used in connection with any of the above-mentioned items. Also disallows a deduction for expenses associated with providing any qualified transportation fringe benefit to the taxpayer's employees. Employers may still deduct 50% of the food and beverage expenses associated with operating their trade or business (e.g., meals consumed by employees on work travel). TCJA eliminated the deductions for certain entertainment expenses but retained the 50 percent deduction for meals (food and beverages) through 2025. We will discuss this in more details below.

Meals

Under the act, taxpayers are still generally able to deduct 50% of the food and beverage expenses associated with operating their trade or business. Business meals provided for the convenience of the employer are now only 50% deductible, whereas before the act they were fully deductible. Barring further action by Congress, those meals will be nondeductible after 2025. Businesses must continue to account for meals and entertainment expenses by classification in order to apply the appropriate limitation, with the addition of a new category in 2018 for "entertainment meals". A comprehensive chart is provided below, to summarize proper treatment for many types of meals and entertainment expenditures, under the law applicable both before and after the act. Take a look at the chart below to see how the new reform has tweaked the business meals and entertainment deduction.

Business Meals and Entertainment	Pre-Reform	Tax Cuts & Jobs Act
Client Entertainment and/or Client Entertainment Meals	50% deduction	No deduction allowed for an activity generally considered to be entertainment, amusement or recreation. No membership dues with respect to any club organized for business, pleasure, recreation or other social purposes. No deduction for meals incurred when no business is conducted (e.g. meals incurred at night clubs, lounges, theaters, country clubs, golf courses, sporting events, vacations and other similar type of events and venues)
Client Business Meals	50% deduction	50% deduction
Employee Travel Meals	50% deduction	50% deduction
Meals for Convenience of Employer	100% if de minimis fringe benefit	50% deductible (0% after 2025 for eating facility**)
Office Holiday Party or Picnic	100% deduction	100% deduction

Charitable Sporting Events Tickets	100% deduction	No deduction
Meals included in Charitable Sports Package	100% deduction	50% deduction
Water, Coffee and Snacks at the Office	100% deduction	50% deduction
Meals during business travel	50% deduction	50% deduction

Chapter 10

Employment Impact

Since the passing of the TCJA you can't help but notice all the "Now Hiring "signs everywhere you go. According to the Bureau of Labor Statistics, the U.S. unemployment rate has dropped to 3.9 percent, the lowest it has been in 17 years. One of the most fundamental features of the Tax Cuts and Jobs Act is that it lowers the individual income tax rates which then enables small business owners to pay less tax. The reduction in individual tax rates for the small business owners enables them to save money that would have been used to pay toward taxes. Ultimatiely, a decrease in employer taxes translates into increased hiring and lower unemployment rates. According to Factcheck.org, a nonprofit, non-partisan website that describes itself as a "consumer advocate for voters, there has been a gain of nearly 1.5 million unfilled job openings since January 2017.

Here are some noticeable highlights of how the Tax Cuts and Jobs Act has affected employment:

- The jobless rate dropped to the lowest in nearly half a century, and the number of unfilled job openings hit a record high.
- Economic growth spurted to a 4.2 percent annual rate in the most recent quarter.
- Median household income rose to the highest level ever recorded in 2017.
- Total nonfarm employment grew by 3.8 million
- The number of coal mining jobs went up by only 500. Manufacturing jobs grew just a bit faster than total employment.
- Corporate profits and stock prices hit new records.
- The economy added 3.2 million jobs, unemployment fell to the lowest level in 18 years, and the number of job openings grew larger than the number of job-seekers for the first time on record.
- Inflation-adjusted weekly wages rose 1.2 percent.
- Home prices rose 17 percent, to a record level.
- New employer tax credit for paid family and medical leave available for 2018 and 2019

Chapter 11

Paycheck Checkup

You may be wondering what to expect and what moves you should make now since the Tax Cuts and Jobs Act has been implemented. One of the most important moves you can make is to do a paycheck checkup. The Tax Cuts and Jobs Act changed the way taxable income is calculated and reduced the tax rates on that income which means many wage earners withholding went down and you may be seeing more money in your paycheck because of the lower tax rates under the new law. A paycheck checkup can help protect you against unpleasant tax surprises that are result of having too little tax withheld and help you avoid facing an unexpected tax bill.

The IRS updated withholding tables with the new rates for employers to use during 2018. Employers began using the new withholding tables February. 15, 2018. Under the new rules, individual tax rates are being lowered to 10%, 12%, 22%, 24%, 32%, 35% and 37%, and these new rates will be reflected in the amount of money being withheld from your 2018 paychecks, as well as your tax liability for 2018. The IRS is urging everyone to check their withholding, The IRS is encouraging taxpayers to use the Withholding Calculator, found on the IRS website at www.irs.gov/individuals/irs-withholding-calculator, to perform a Paycheck Checkup to help determine if they need to adjust their withholding or make estimated or additional tax payments now. This helpful tool along with IRS Publication 505, *Tax Withholding and Estimated Tax,* can help you calculate credits and help you determine the correct amount of withholding that should be taken out of your paycheck due to the tax reform.

Because these changes apply to the individual section of the tax code, employers had to adjust their income tax withholding for employees and were required by the IRS to implement new withholding tables. Changes in the new law, such as elimination of exemptions, changes in available itemized deductions, increases in the Child Tax Credit and the new dependent credit are not reflected in the revised withholding tables for 2018 and will impact your withholding on your paycheck. Because of all of changes in the TCJA, refunds may be different than prior years for certain taxpayers. Be aware that you may receive a smaller refund - or even owe an unexpected tax bill – when you file your 2018 tax return especially if you did not adjust Form W-4 after the withholding tables changed.

Form W-4 (Employee's Withholding Allowance Certificate) is completed and submitted to your employer so they know how much tax to withhold from your pay. Typically, you would file a new W-4 when your personal or financial situation changes however you should check your withholding often and adjust it when your situation changes any time of the year.

In the next and final chapter, you will have an opportunity to see illustrations of the changes to Form W-4, *Employee's Withholding Allowance Certificate*, along with drafts of the proposed new 1040 and proposed schedules.

Chapter 12

Make Forms Great Again

The IRS revised the W-4 form to reflect additional changes in the new law. Because the TCJA increased the standard deduction, increased the credit for child tax, repealed exemptions, limited certain deductions and changed the tax rates and brackets, the IRS has issued a draft version of the 2019 Form W-4, *Employee's Withholding Allowance Certificate,* along with the instructions for the form that can be found at https:// www.irs.gov/pub/irs-dft/fw4--dft.pdf. NOTE: Beware that the IRS advises that taxpayers should NOT rely on draft forms, instructions, and publications for filing. The draft forms displayed in this chapter are for informational purposes only. The IRS stated that they provided the draft forms as a courtesy, and though it does not usually release draft forms until it has incorporated all changes.

As a result of the Tax Cuts & Jobs Act, The IRS has announced changes to the main tax forms for the 2018 tax year. The IRS has consolidated all the old individual 1040 tax forms (1040 Long, 1040A and1040EZ) into a postcard sized form. The thought was that this would help to simplify the daunting task of doing your taxes but this remains to be seen. In addition to shortening the Form 1040 to a postcard-sized return, the IRS has added six new schedules that will support the new 1040. Although the forms have not been finalized, as of the printing of this book, you can take a look on the following pages to see what the IRS has proposed for the W-4, the new 1040 and Schedules 1 – 6.

Caution: *DRAFT—NOT FOR FILING*

This is an early release draft of the 2018 IRS Form 1040, U.S. Individual Income Tax Return, which the IRS is providing for your information, review, and comment. **Do not file draft forms.** Also, do **not** rely on draft forms, instructions, and publications for filing. We generally do not release drafts of forms until we believe we have incorporated all changes, and we do not expect this draft to change significantly before being published as final. Forms generally are subject to OMB approval before they can be officially released. Early release drafts are at IRS.gov/DraftForms, and may remain there even after the final release is posted at IRS.gov/LatestForms. All information about forms, instructions, and publications is at IRS.gov/Forms.

Also, note that almost every form and publication also has its own page on IRS.gov. For example, the Form 1040 page is at IRS.gov/Form1040; a Form W-8BEN-E page is at IRS.gov/W8BENE; the Publication 17 page is at IRS.gov/Pub17; the Form W-4 page is at IRS.gov/W4; and the Schedule A (Form 1040) page is at IRS.gov/ScheduleA. If typing in a link instead of clicking on it, be sure to type the link into the address bar of your browser, not in a Search box. Note that these are friendly shortcut links that will automatically redirect to the actual link for the page.

If you wish, you can submit comments about this draft Form 1040 and/or its 6 new numbered schedules to WI.1040.Comments@IRS.gov. We cannot respond to all comments due to the high volume we receive. Please note that we may not be able to consider some suggestions until the 2019 revisions.

Form Changes

The IRS announced changes to the main tax form for tax year 2018. They consolidated the 1040 Long, 1040EZ, and 1040A into one 1040 Form that all individual filers will use.

SCHEDULE 1 (Form 1040)	Additional Income and Adjustments to Income	OMB No. 1545-0074
Department of the Treasury Internal Revenue Service	► Attach to Form 1040. ► Go to *www.irs.gov/Form1040* for instructions and the latest information.	2018 Attachment Sequence No. 01

Name(s) shown on Form 1040	Your social security number

Additional Income	**1–9b**	Reserved	**1–9b**	
	10	Taxable refunds, credits, or offsets of state and local income taxes	10	
	11	Alimony received	11	
	12	Business income or (loss). Attach Schedule C or C-EZ	12	
	13	Capital gain or (loss). Attach Schedule D if required. If not required, check here ► ☐	13	
	14	Other gains or (losses). Attach Form 4797	14	
	15a	Reserved	15b	
	16a	Reserved	16b	
	17	Rental real estate, royalties, partnerships, S corporations, trusts, etc. Attach Schedule E	17	
	18	Farm income or (loss). Attach Schedule F	18	
	19	Unemployment compensation	19	
	20a	Reserved	20b	
	21	Other income. List type and amount ►	21	
	22	Combine the amounts in the far right column. If you don't have any adjustments to income, enter here and include on Form 1040, line 6. Otherwise, go to line 23	22	

Adjustments to Income	23	Educator expenses	23		
	24	Certain business expenses of reservists, performing artists, and fee-basis government officials. Attach Form 2106	24		
	25	Health savings account deduction. Attach Form 8889	25		
	26	Moving expenses for members of the Armed Forces. Attach Form 3903	26		
	27	Deductible part of self-employment tax. Attach Schedule SE	27		
	28	Self-employed SEP, SIMPLE, and qualified plans	28		
	29	Self-employed health insurance deduction	29		
	30	Penalty on early withdrawal of savings	30		
	31a	Alimony paid b Recipient's SSN ►	31a		
	32	IRA deduction	32		
	33	Student loan interest deduction	33		
	34	Reserved	34		
	35	Reserved	35		
	36	Add lines 23 through 35	36		

For Paperwork Reduction Act Notice, see your tax return instructions.   Cat. No. 71479F   Schedule 1 (Form 1040) 2018

SCHEDULE 2
(Form 1040)

Department of the Treasury
Internal Revenue Service

Tax

▶ Attach to Form 1040.
▶ Go to *www.irs.gov/Form1040* for instructions and the latest information.

OMB No. 1545-0074

20**18**

Attachment
Sequence No. **02**

Name(s) shown on Form 1040

Your social security number

Tax	38–44	Reserved	38–44	
	45	Alternative minimum tax. Attach Form 6251	45	
	46	Excess advance premium tax credit repayment. Attach Form 8962	46	
	47	Add the amounts in the far right column. Enter here and include on Form 1040, line 11	47	

For Paperwork Reduction Act Notice, see your tax return instructions.

Cat. No. 71478U

Schedule 2 (Form 1040) 2018

DRAFT AS OF
July 31, 2018
DO NOT FILE

SCHEDULE 3
(Form 1040)

Department of the Treasury
Internal Revenue Service

Nonrefundable Credits

▶ Attach to Form 1040.
▶ Go to *www.irs.gov/Form1040* for instructions and the latest information.

OMB No. 1545-0074

20**18**

Attachment
Sequence No. **03**

Name(s) shown on Form 1040

Your social security number

Nonrefundable Credits	48	Foreign tax credit. Attach Form 1116 if required	48	
	49	Credit for child and dependent care expenses. Attach Form 2441	49	
	50	Education credits from Form 8863, line 19	50	
	51	Retirement savings contributions credit. Attach Form 8880	51	
	52	Reserved	52	
	53	Residential energy credit. Attach Form 5695	53	
	54	Other credits from Form **a** ☐ 3800 **b** ☐ 8801 **c** ☐ _____	54	
	55	Add the amounts in the far right column. Enter here and include on Form 1040, line 12	55	

For Paperwork Reduction Act Notice, see your tax return instructions. Cat. No. 71480G Schedule 3 (Form 1040) 2018

48

SCHEDULE 4
(Form 1040)

Department of the Treasury
Internal Revenue Service

Other Taxes

▶ Attach to Form 1040.
▶ Go to *www.irs.gov/Form1040* for instructions and the latest information.

OMB No. 1545-0074

2018

Attachment
Sequence No. **04**

Name(s) shown on Form 1040

Your social security number

Other Taxes	57	Self-employment tax. Attach Schedule SE	57	
	58	Unreported social security and Medicare tax from: Form **a** ☐ 4137 **b** ☐ 8919	58	
	59	Additional tax on IRAs, other qualified retirement plans, and other tax-favored accounts. Attach Form 5329 if required	59	
	60a	Household employment taxes. Attach Schedule H	60a	
	b	Repayment of first-time homebuyer credit from Form 5405. Attach Form 5405 if required	60b	
	61	Health care: individual responsibility (see instructions)	61	
	62	Taxes from: **a** ☐ Form 8959 **b** ☐ Form 8960 **c** ☐ Instructions; enter code(s)	62	
	63	Section 965 net tax liability installment from Form 965-A 63		
	64	Add the amounts in the far right column. These are your **total other taxes.** Enter here and on Form 1040, line 14	64	

For Paperwork Reduction Act Notice, see your tax return instructions.

Cat. No. 71481R

Schedule 4 (Form 1040) 2018

49

SCHEDULE 5
(Form 1040)

Department of the Treasury
Internal Revenue Service

Other Payments and Refundable Credits

▶ Attach to Form 1040.
▶ Go to *www.irs.gov/Form1040* for instructions and the latest information.

OMB No. 1545-0074

2018
Attachment
Sequence No. **05**

Name(s) shown on Form 1040

Your social security number

Other Payments and Refundable Credits	65	Reserved	65	
	66	2018 estimated tax payments and amount applied from 2017 return . .	66	
	67a	Reserved	67a	
	b	Reserved	67b	
	68–69	Reserved	68–69	
	70	Net premium tax credit. Attach Form 8962	70	
	71	Amount paid with request for extension to file (see instructions) . . .	71	
	72	Excess social security and tier 1 RRTA tax withheld	72	
	73	Credit for federal tax on fuels. Attach Form 4136	73	
	74	Credits from Form: **a** ☐ 2439 **b** ☐ Reserved **c** ☐ 8885 **d** ☐ _____	74	
	75	Add the amounts in the far right column. These are your total **other payments and refundable credits.** Enter here and include on Form 1040, line 17	75	

For Paperwork Reduction Act Notice, see your tax return instructions.

Cat. No. 71482C

Schedule 5 (Form 1040) 2018

SCHEDULE 6
(Form 1040)

Department of the Treasury
Internal Revenue Service

Foreign Address and Third Party Designee

► Attach to Form 1040.
► Go to *www.irs.gov/Form1040* for instructions and the latest information.

OMB No. 1545-0074

2018

Attachment
Sequence No. **05A**

Name(s) shown on Form 1040

Your social security number

Foreign Address	Foreign country name	Foreign province/county	Foreign postal code

Third Party Designee	Do you want to allow another person to discuss this return with the IRS (see instructions)? ☐ **Yes.** Complete below. ☐ **No**
	Designee's name ► Phone no. ► Personal identification number (PIN) ►

For Paperwork Reduction Act Notice, see your tax return instructions.

Cat. No. 71483N

Schedule 6 (Form 1040) 2018

51

Caution: *DRAFT—NOT FOR FILING*

This is an early release draft of an IRS tax form, instructions, or publication, which the IRS is providing for your information as a courtesy. **Do not file draft forms.** Also, do **not** rely on draft forms, instructions, and publications for filing. We generally do not release drafts of forms until we believe we have incorporated all changes. However, unexpected issues sometimes arise, or legislation is passed, necessitating a change to a draft form. In addition, forms generally are subject to OMB approval before they can be officially released. Drafts of instructions and publications usually have at least some changes before being officially released.

Early release drafts are at IRS.gov/DraftForms, and may remain there even after the final release is posted at IRS.gov/DownloadForms. All information about all forms, instructions, and pubs is at IRS.gov/Forms.

Almost every form and publication also has its own page on IRS.gov. For example, the Form 1040 page is at IRS.gov/Form1040; the Publication 17 page is at IRS.gov/Pub17; the Form W-4 page is at IRS.gov/W4; and the Schedule A (Form 1040) page is at IRS.gov/ScheduleA. If typing in a link above instead of clicking on it, be sure to type the link into the address bar of your browser, not in a Search box. Note that these are friendly shortcut links that will automatically go to the actual link for the page.

If you wish, you can submit comments about draft or final forms, instructions, or publications at IRS.gov/FormsComments. We cannot respond to all comments due to the high volume we receive. Please note that we may not be able to consider many suggestions until the subsequent revision of the product.

Form W-4 (2019)

Future developments. For the latest information about any future developments related to Form W-4, such as legislation enacted after it was published, go to *www.irs.gov/FormW4*.

Purpose. Complete Form W-4 so that your employer can withhold the correct federal income tax from your pay. Consider completing a new Form W-4 each year and when your personal or financial situation changes.

Exemption from withholding. You may claim exemption from withholding for 2019 if **both** of the following apply.

• For 2018 you had a right to a refund of **all** federal income tax withheld because you had **no** tax liability, **and**

• For 2019 you expect a refund of **all** federal income tax withheld because you expect to have **no** tax liability.

If you're exempt, complete **only** lines 1, 2, 3, 4, and 7 and sign the form to validate it. Your exemption for 2019 expires February 17, 2020. See Pub. 505, Tax Withholding and Estimated Tax, to learn more about whether you qualify for exemption from withholding.

General Instructions

If you aren't exempt, follow the rest of these instructions to determine the number of withholding allowances you should claim for withholding for 2019 and any additional amount of tax to have withheld. For regular wages, withholding must be based on allowances you claimed and may not be a flat amount or percentage of wages.

You can also use the calculator at *www.irs.gov/W4App* to determine your tax withholding more accurately. Consider using this calculator if you have a more complicated tax situation, such as if you have a working spouse, more than one job, or a large amount of nonwage income not subject to withholding outside of your job. After your Form W-4 takes effect, you can also use this calculator to see how the amount of tax you're having withheld compares to your projected total tax for 2019. If you use the calculator, you don't need to complete any of the worksheets for Form W-4.

Note that if you have too much tax withheld, you will receive a refund when you file your tax return. If you have too little tax withheld, you will owe tax when you file your tax return, and you might owe a penalty.

Filers with multiple jobs or working spouses. If you have more than one job at a time, or if you're married filing jointly and your spouse is also working, read all of the instructions including the instructions for the Two-Earners/Multiple Jobs Worksheet before beginning.

Nonwage income. If you have a large amount of nonwage income not subject to withholding, such as interest or dividends, consider making estimated tax payments using Form 1040-ES, Estimated Tax for Individuals. Otherwise, you might owe additional tax. Or, you can use the Deductions, Adjustments, and Other Income Worksheet on page 3 or the calculator at *www.irs.gov/W4App* to make sure you have enough tax withheld from your paycheck. If you have pension or annuity income, see Pub. 505 or use the calculator at *www.irs.gov/W4App* to find out if you should adjust your withholding on Form W-4 or W-4P.

Nonresident alien. If you're a nonresident alien, see Notice 1392, Supplemental Form W-4 Instructions for Nonresident Aliens, before completing this form.

Specific Instructions

Personal Allowances Worksheet

Complete this worksheet on page 3 first to determine the number of withholding allowances to claim.

Line C. *Head of household please note:* Generally, you may claim head of household filing status on your tax return only if you're unmarried and pay more than 50% of the costs of keeping up a home for yourself and a qualifying individual. See Pub. 501 for more information about filing status.

Line E. Child tax credit. When you file your tax return, you may be eligible to claim a child tax credit for each of your eligible children. To qualify, the child must be under age 17 as of December 31, must be your dependent who lives with you for more than half the year, and must have a valid social security number. To learn more about this credit, see Pub. 972, Child Tax Credit. To reduce the tax withheld from your pay by taking this credit into account, follow the instructions on line E of the worksheet. On the worksheet you will be asked about your total income. For this purpose, total income includes all of your wages and other income, including income earned by a spouse if you are filing a joint return.

Line F. Credit for other dependents. When you file your tax return, you may be eligible to claim a credit for other dependents for whom a child tax credit can't be claimed, such as a qualifying child who doesn't meet the age or social security number requirement for the child tax credit, or a qualifying relative. To learn more about this credit, see Pub. 972. To reduce the tax withheld from your pay by taking this credit into account, follow the instructions on line F of the worksheet. On the worksheet, you will be asked about your total income. For this purpose, total

---

Separate here and give Form W-4 to your employer. Keep the worksheet(s) for your records.

Form **W-4**	**Employee's Withholding Allowance Certificate**	OMB No. 1545-0074
Department of the Treasury Internal Revenue Service	► Whether you're entitled to claim a certain number of allowances or exemption from withholding is subject to review by the IRS. Your employer may be required to send a copy of this form to the IRS.	**2019**

1 Your first name and middle initial	Last name	2 Your social security number

Home address (number and street or rural route)

3 ☐ Single ☐ Married ☐ Married, but withhold at higher Single rate.
Note: If married filing separately, check "Married, but withhold at higher Single rate."

City or town, state, and ZIP code

4 If your last name differs from that shown on your social security card, check here. You must call 800-772-1213 for a replacement card. ► ☐

5	Total number of allowances you're claiming (from the applicable worksheet on the following pages)	5	
6	Additional amount, if any, you want withheld from each paycheck	6	$

7 I claim exemption from withholding for 2019, and I certify that I meet **both** of the following conditions for exemption.

• Last year I had a right to a refund of **all** federal income tax withheld because I had **no** tax liability, **and**

• This year I expect a refund of **all** federal income tax withheld because I expect to have **no** tax liability.

If you meet both conditions, write "Exempt" here . . . . ► 7

Under penalties of perjury, I declare that I have examined this certificate and, to the best of my knowledge and belief, it is true, correct, and complete.

Employee's signature
(This form is not valid unless you sign it.) ►   Date ►

8 Employer's name and address (**Employer:** Complete boxes 8 and 10 if sending to IRS and complete boxes 8, 9, and 10 if sending to State Directory of New Hires.)	9 First date of employment	10 Employer identification number (EIN)

For Privacy Act and Paperwork Reduction Act Notice, see page 4.   Cat. No. 10220Q   Form **W-4** (2019)

income includes all of your wages and other income, including income earned by a spouse if you are filing a joint return.

Line G. Other credits. You may be able to reduce the tax withheld from your paycheck if you expect to claim other tax credits, such as tax credits for education (see Pub. 970). If you do so, your paycheck will be larger, but the amount of any refund that you receive when you file your tax return will be smaller. Follow the instructions for Worksheet 1-6 in Pub. 505 if you want to reduce your withholding to take these credits into account. Enter "-0-" on lines E and F if you use Worksheet 1-6.

Deductions, Adjustments, and Additional Income Worksheet

Complete this worksheet to determine if you're able to reduce the tax withheld from your paycheck to account for your itemized deductions and other adjustments to income, such as IRA contributions. If you do so, your refund at the end of the year will be smaller, but your paycheck will be larger. You're not required to complete this worksheet or reduce your withholding if you don't wish to do so.

You can also use this worksheet to figure out how much to increase the tax withheld from your paycheck if you have a large amount of nonwage income not subject to withholding, such as interest or dividends.

Another option is to take these items into account and make your withholding more accurate by using the calculator at *www.irs.gov/W4App*. If you use the calculator, you don't need to complete any of the worksheets for Form W-4.

Two-Earners/Multiple Jobs Worksheet

Complete this worksheet if you have more than one job at a time or are married filing jointly and have a working spouse. If you

don't complete this worksheet, you might have too little tax withheld. If so, you will owe tax when you file your tax return and might be subject to a penalty.

Figure the total number of allowances you're entitled to claim and any additional amount of tax to withhold on all jobs using worksheets from only one Form W-4. Claim all allowances on the W-4 that you or your spouse file for the highest paying job in your family and claim zero allowances on Forms W-4 filed for all other jobs. For example, if you earn $60,000 per year and your spouse earns $20,000, you should complete the worksheets to determine what to enter on lines 5 and 6 of your Form W-4, and your spouse should enter zero ("-0-") on lines 5 and 6 of his or her Form W-4. See Pub. 505 for details.

Another option is to use the calculator at *www.irs.gov/W4App* to make your withholding more accurate.

Tip: If you have a working spouse and your incomes are similar, you can check the "Married, but withhold at higher Single rate" box instead of using this worksheet. If you choose this option, then each spouse should fill out the Personal Allowances Worksheet and check the "Married, but withhold at higher Single rate" box on Form W-4, but only one spouse should claim any allowances for credits or fill out the Deductions, Adjustments, and Additional Income Worksheet.

Instructions for Employer

Employees, do not complete box 8, 9, or 10. Your employer will complete these boxes if necessary.

New hire reporting. Employers are required by law to report new employees to a designated State Directory of New Hires. Employers may use Form W-4, boxes 8, 9,

and 10 to comply with the new hire reporting requirement for a newly hired employee. A newly hired employee is an employee who hasn't previously been employed by the employer, or who was previously employed by the employer but has been separated from such prior employment for at least 60 consecutive days. Employers should contact the appropriate State Directory of New Hires to find out how to submit a copy of the completed Form W-4. For information and links to each designated State Directory of New Hires (including for U.S. territories), go to *www.acf.hhs.gov/css/employers*.

If an employer is sending a copy of Form W-4 to a designated State Directory of New Hires to comply with the new hire reporting requirement for a newly hired employee, complete boxes 8, 9, and 10 as follows.

Box 8. Enter the employer's name and address. If the employer is sending a copy of this form to a State Directory of New Hires, enter the address where child support agencies should send income withholding orders.

Box 9. If the employer is sending a copy of this form to a State Directory of New Hires, enter the employee's first date of employment, which is the date services for payment were first performed by the employee. If the employer rehired the employee after the employee had been separated from the employer's service for at least 60 days, enter the rehire date.

Box 10. Enter the employer's employer identification number (EIN).

Personal Allowances Worksheet (Keep for your records.)

A	Enter "1" for yourself	**A** ____
B	Enter "1" if you will file as married filing jointly	**B** ____
C	Enter "1" if you will file as head of household	**C** ____

D Enter "1" if:
- You're single, or married filing separately, and have only one job; or
- You're married filing jointly, have only one job, and your spouse doesn't work; or
- Your wages from a second job or your spouse's wages (or the total of both) are $X,XXX or less.

D ____

E **Child tax credit.** See Pub. 972, Child Tax Credit, for more information.
- If your total income will be less than $XX,XXX ($XXX,XXX if married filing jointly), enter "4" for each eligible child.
- If your total income will be from $XX,XXX to $XXX,XXX ($XXX,XXX to $XXX,XXX if married filing jointly), enter "2" for each eligible child.
- If your total income will be from $XXX,XXX to $XXX,XXX ($XXX,XXX to $XXX,XXX if married filing jointly), enter "1" for each eligible child.
- If your total income will be higher than $200,000 ($400,000 if married filing jointly), enter "-0-".

E ____

F **Credit for other dependents.** See Pub. 972, Child Tax Credit, for more information.
- If your total income will be less than $XX,XXX ($XXX,XXX if married filing jointly), enter "1" for each eligible dependent.
- If your total income will be from $XX,XXX to $XXX,XXX ($XXX,XXX to $XXX,XXX if married filing jointly), enter "1" for every two dependents (for example, "-0-" for one dependent, "1" if you have two dependents, and "2" if you have four dependents).
- If your total income will be higher than $XXX,XXX ($XXX,XXX if married filing jointly), enter "-0-". . . . .

F ____

G **Other credits.** If you have other credits, see Worksheet 1-6 of Pub. 505 and enter the amount from that worksheet here. If you use Worksheet 1-6, enter "-0-" on lines E and F . . . .

G ____

H Add lines A through G and enter the total here . . . . ▶ **H** ____

For accuracy, complete all worksheets that apply.	• If you plan to **itemize** or **claim adjustments to income** and want to reduce your withholding, or if you have a large amount of nonwage income not subject to withholding and want to increase your withholding, see the **Deductions, Adjustments, and Additional Income Worksheet** below.
	• If you **have more than one job at a time** or are **married filing jointly and you and your spouse both work**, and the combined earnings from all jobs exceed $XX,XXX ($XX,XXX if married filing jointly), see the **Two-Earners/Multiple Jobs Worksheet** on page 4 to avoid having too little tax withheld.
	• If **neither** of the above situations applies, **stop here** and enter the number from line H on line 5 of Form W-4 above.

Deductions, Adjustments, and Additional Income Worksheet

Note: Use this worksheet *only* if you plan to itemize deductions, claim certain adjustments to income, or have a large amount of nonwage income not subject to withholding.

1	Enter an estimate of your 2019 itemized deductions. These include qualifying home mortgage interest, charitable contributions, state and local taxes (up to $10,000), and medical expenses in excess of 10% of your income. See Pub. 505 for details	1 $ ____
2	Enter: $XX,XXX if you're married filing jointly or qualifying widow(er) $XX,XXX if you're head of household $XX,XXX if you're single or married filing separately	2 $ ____
3	**Subtract** line 2 from line 1. If zero or less, enter "-0-"	3 $ ____
4	Enter an estimate of your 2019 adjustments to income, qualified business income deduction, and any additional standard deduction for age or blindness (see Pub. 505 for information about these items) . .	4 $ ____
5	**Add** lines 3 and 4 and enter the total	5 $ ____
6	Enter an estimate of your 2019 nonwage income not subject to withholding (such as dividends or interest) .	6 $ ____
7	**Subtract** line 6 from line 5. If zero, enter "-0-". If less than zero, enter the amount in parentheses . . .	7 $ ____
8	**Divide** the amount on line 7 by $X,XXX and enter the result here. If a negative amount, enter in parentheses. Drop any fraction	8 ____
9	Enter the number from the **Personal Allowances Worksheet**, line H, above	9 ____
10	**Add** lines 8 and 9 and enter the total here. If zero or less, enter "-0-". If you plan to use the **Two-Earners/ Multiple Jobs Worksheet**, also enter this total on line 1 of that worksheet on page 4. Otherwise, **stop here** and enter this total on Form W-4, line 5, page 1	10 ____

Two-Earners/Multiple Jobs Worksheet

Note: Use this worksheet *only* if the instructions under line H from the **Personal Allowances Worksheet** direct you here.

1   Enter the number from the **Personal Allowances Worksheet**, line H, page 3 (or, if you used the **Deductions, Adjustments, and Additional Income Worksheet** on page 3, the number from line 10 of that worksheet) . . . . **1** _____

2   Find the number in **Table 1** below that applies to the **LOWEST** paying job and enter it here. **However,** if you're married filing jointly and wages from the highest paying job are $XX,XXX or less and the combined wages for you and your spouse are $XXX,XXX or less, don't enter more than "3" . . . . **2** _____

3   If line 1 is **more than or equal to** line 2, subtract line 2 from line 1. Enter the result here (if zero, enter "-0-") and on Form W-4, line 5, page 1. **Do not** use the rest of this worksheet . . . . **3** _____

Note: If line 1 is **less than** line 2, enter "-0-" on Form W-4, line 5, page 1. Complete lines 4 through 9 below to figure the additional withholding amount necessary to avoid a year-end tax bill.

4   Enter the number from line 2 of this worksheet . . . . **4** _____
5   Enter the number from line 1 of this worksheet . . . . **5** _____
6   **Subtract** line 5 from line 4 . . . . **6** _____
7   Find the amount in **Table 2** below that applies to the **HIGHEST** paying job and enter it here . . . . **7** $_____
8   **Multiply** line 7 by line 6 and enter the result here. This is the additional annual withholding needed . . . **8** $_____
9   **Divide** line 8 by the number of pay periods remaining in 2019. For example, divide by 18 if you're paid every 2 weeks and you complete this form on a date in late April when there are 18 pay periods remaining in 2019. Enter the result here and on Form W-4, line 6, page 1. This is the additional amount to be withheld from each paycheck . . . . **9** $_____

Table 1				Table 2			
Married Filing Jointly		**All Others**		**Married Filing Jointly**		**All Others**	
If wages from **LOWEST** paying job are—	Enter on line 2 above	If wages from **LOWEST** paying job are—	Enter on line 2 above	If wages from **HIGHEST** paying job are—	Enter on line 7 above	If wages from **HIGHEST** paying job are—	Enter on line 7 above
$X - $X,XXX	0	$X - $X,XXX	0	$X - $XX,XXX	$XXX	$X - $X,XXX	$XXX
X,XXX - X,XXX	1	X,XXX - XX,XXX	1	XX,XXX - XX,XXX	XXX	X,XXX - XX,XXX	XXX
X,XXX - XX,XXX	2	XX,XXX - XX,XXX	2	XX,XXX - XXX,XXX	XXX	XX,XXX - XX,XXX	XXX
XX,XXX - XX,XXX	3	XX,XXX - XX,XXX	3	XXX,XXX - XXX,XXX	X,XXX	XX,XXX - XXX,XXX	X,XXX
XX,XXX - XX,XXX	4	XX,XXX - XX,XXX	4	XXX,XXX - XXX,XXX	X,XXX	XXX,XXX - XXX,XXX	X,XXX
XX,XXX - XX,XXX	5	XX,XXX - XX,XXX	5	XXX,XXX - XXX,XXX	X,XXX	XXX,XXX - XXX,XXX	X,XXX
XX,XXX - XX,XXX	6	XX,XXX - XX,XXX	6	XXX,XXX and over	X,XXX	XXX,XXX and over	X,XXX
XX,XXX - XX,XXX	7	XX,XXX - XX,XXX	7				
XX,XXX - XX,XXX	8	XX,XXX - XX,XXX	8				
XX,XXX - XX,XXX	9	XX,XXX - XXX,XXX	9				
XX,XXX - X,XXX	10	XXX,XXX - XXX,XXX	10				
XX,XXX - XX,XXX	11	XXX,XXX - XXX,XXX	11				
XX,XXX - XXX,XXX	12	XXX,XXX - XXX,XXX	12				
XXX,XXX - XXX,XXX	13	XXX,XXX - XXX,XXX	13				
XXX,XXX - XXX,XXX	14	XXX,XXX - XXX,XXX	14				
XXX,XXX - XXX,XXX	15	XXX,XXX - XXX,XXX	15				
XXX,XXX - XXX,XXX	16	XXX,XXX - XXX,XXX	16				
XXX,XXX - XXX,XXX	17	XXX,XXX and over	17				
XXX,XXX - XXX,XXX	18						
XXX,XXX and over	19						

56

Below is an illustration of the changes between the 2017 form and updated 2018 revision.

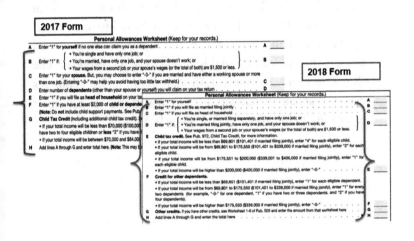

2017 Form

Personal Allowances Worksheet (Keep for your records.)

A Enter "1" for yourself if no one else can claim you as a dependent . . . . A ____

B Enter "1" if:
- You're single and have only one job; or
- You're married, have only one job, and your spouse doesn't work; or
- Your wages from a second job or your spouse's wages (or the total of both) are $1,500 or less.
B ____

C Enter "1" for your **spouse**. But, you may choose to enter "-0-" if you are married and have either a working spouse or more than one job. (Entering "-0-" may help you avoid having too little tax withheld.) . . . . C ____

D Enter number of **dependents** (other than your spouse or yourself) you will claim on your tax return . . . . D ____

E Enter "1" if you will file as **head of household** on your ta

F Enter "1" if you have at least $2,000 of **child or depende**
(Note: Do not include child support payments. See Pub

G **Child Tax Credit** (including additional child tax credit).
- If your total income will be less than $70,000 ($100,00
have two to four eligible children or **less** "2" if you have
- If your total income will be between $70,000 and $84,00

H Add lines A through G and enter total here. (Note: This may b

2018 Form

Personal Allowances Worksheet (Keep for your records.)

A Enter "1" for yourself . . . . A ____

B Enter "1" if you will file as married filing jointly . . . . B ____

C Enter "1" if you will file as head of household . . . . C ____

D Enter "1" if:
- You're single, or married filing separately, and have only one job; or
- You're married filing jointly, have only one job, and your spouse doesn't work; or
- Your wages from a second job or your spouse's wages (or the total of both) are $1,500 or less.
D ____

E **Child tax credit.** See Pub. 972, Child Tax Credit, for more information.
- If your total income will be less than $69,801 ($101,401 if married filing jointly), enter "4" for each eligible child.
- If your total income will be from $69,801 to $175,550 ($101,401 to $339,000 if married filing jointly), enter "2" for each eligible child.
- If your total income will be from $175,551 to $200,000 ($339,001 to $400,000 if married filing jointly), enter "1" for each eligible child.
- If your total income will be higher than $200,000 ($400,000 if married filing jointly), enter "-0-" . . . . E ____

F **Credit for other dependents.**
- If your total income will be less than $69,801 ($101,401 if married filing jointly), enter "1" for each eligible dependent.
- If your total income will be from $69,801 to $175,550 ($101,401 to $339,000 if married filing jointly), enter "1" for every two dependents (for example, "-0-" for one dependent, "1" if you have two or three dependents, and "2" if you have four dependents).
- If your total income will be higher than $175,550 ($339,000 if married filing jointly), enter "-0-" . . . . F ____

G **Other credits.** If you have other credits, see Worksheet 1-6 of Pub. 505 and enter the amount from that worksheet here . . G ____

H Add lines A through G and enter the total here . . . . H ____

Summary

It's important that you look at Publication, 5307, *Tax Reform Basics for Individuals and Families*. This is the IRS' effort in assisting you your 2018 tax return. However, if the new reform gets to be a little overwhelming or even if you just want to get clarity on certain aspects of the reform, I always recommend seeking the advice of a highly trained tax professional. The IRS website has the most up-to-date information about tax reform that can be found at https://www.irs.gov/tax-reform or by visiting Publication 5307 at www.IRS.gov/getready.

FAQ

How did the new tax laws change? Will I be paying more or less in taxes?

Everyone's financial situation is different, so tax reform will affect everyone differently. You can learn about the new tax laws and access tools to help you estimate your future tax numbers at the IRS website www.irs.gov/tax-reform.

What is the current status of tax reform? When will new tax laws take effect?

While most of the changes from the plan went into effect on January 1, 2018 some parts of the tax plan are retroactive. There are also a couple of changes that won't take full effect until 2019.

How do 2018 tax reform changes affect my self-employed business?

There is a 20% deduction on self-employed income on net business income. The new law allows a brand-new tax deduction for owners of pass-through entities, including partners in partnerships, shareholders in S corporations, members of limited liability companies (LLCs) and sole proprietors. This deduction allows you to keep more earnings tax-free.

Are the tax rates lower?

Yes, the Individual Tax Rates are lower beginning in 2018

Do I need to file a new Form W-4 with my employer?

Because of the changes to the 2018 tax laws, such as changes to itemized deductions, increased child tax credit to $2,000, the new dependent credit, and the eliminations of dependent and personal exemptions, you should file a new Form W-4 with your employer in response to the new tax law, if your personal situations changed, or if you started a new job.

Appendix A

Side-by-Side comparison of Pre-reform tax law and the "Tax Cuts and Jobs Act"

PRE-REFORM	TAX CUTS & JOBS ACT (2018)
Exemptions	
$4,050	Suspended through 2025 (effectively repealed)
Standard Deductions	
Single: $6,350	Single: $12,000
Head of household: $9,350	Head of household: $18,000
Married filing joint: $12,700	Married filing joint: $ 24,000
Add'l Elderly & Blind	Add'l Elderly & Blind
Joint & Surviving Spouse: $1,250	Joint & Surviving Spouse: $1,300
Others: $1,550	Others: $1,600
Itemized Deductions	
Medical – Allowed in excess of 10% of AGI	Retained for 2017 and 2018 with an AGI threshold of 7.5% regardless of age. Threshold increases to 10% after 2018. 7.5% threshold also applies for AMT purposes for '17 and '18.

Taxes –Property taxes, and state and local income taxes are deductible. Taxpayers can elect to deduct sales tax in lieu of state income tax.	The deduction for taxes is retained but capped at $10,000 for the year. Foreign real property taxes may not be included. The Act prohibits claiming a 2017 itemized deduction on a pre-payment of income tax for 2018 or other future taxable year in order to avoid the dollar limitation applicable for taxable years beginning after 2017.
Home Mortgage Interest –Allows interest on $1M of acquisition debt on primary and second home and interest on $100K of home equity debt.	Allows interest on $750K of acquisition debt on primary and secondary home. Grandfathers interest on up to $1M of acquisition debt for loans prior to 12/15/2017. Repeals the deduction for home equity debt.
Charitable Contributions – Allows charitable contributions generally not exceeding 50% of a taxpayer's AGI.	Continues to allow charitable contributions and increases the 50% of AGI to 60%. Bans charitable deduction for payments made in exchange for college athletic event seating rights. Also repeals certain substantiation exceptions.
Gambling Losses – Allows a deduction for gambling losses not exceeding gambling income.	Continues to allow a deduction for gambling losses not to exceed the gambling income. Clarifies that "gambling losses" includes any deduction otherwise allowable in carrying on any wagering transaction.
Personal Casualty & Theft Losses – Casualty and theft losses are allowed to the extent each loss exceeds $100 and the sum of all losses for the year exceeds 10% of the taxpayer's AGI.	Suspends personal casualty losses through 2025, except for casualty losses attributable to a disaster declared by the President under Sec 401 of the Robert T Stafford Disaster Relief and Emergency Assistance Act.

Tier 2 Miscellaneous – Includes deductions for employee business expenses, tax preparation fees, investment expenses and certain casualty losses.	Suspends all tier 2 (those subject to the 2% of AGI threshold) itemized deductions through 2025.
Phase-out of Itemized Deductions –Itemized deductions are phased out for higher income taxpayers.	The phase-out is suspended through 2025.
Above-The-Line Deductions	
Teachers' Deduction – Allowed up to $250 (indexed) for classroom supplies and professional development courses.	Continues to allow this deduction.
Moving Deduction & Reimbursements – Allows a deduction for moving expenses for a job-related move where the commute is 50 miles further and the individual is employed for a certain length of time. Qualified moving expense reimbursements are excluded from the employee's gross income.	Deduction is suspended through 2025 except for military change of station. Employer (other than military) reimbursement would be included as taxable wages.
Alimony – Allows the payer of alimony to claim an above-the-line deduction for qualified payments; recipient reports the income.	For divorce agreements entered into after December 31, 2018 or existing agreements modified after that date that specifically include this amendment in the modification, alimony would no longer be deductible by the payer and would not be income to the recipient.

Performing Artists Expenses – An employee with an AGI of $16,000 or less who receives $200 or more from each of two or more employers in the performing arts field can deduct their performing arts expenses that exceed 10% of AGI as an above-the-line deduction.	Retained - The House Bill would have repealed this deduction, but the conference agreement retains it in its current form.
Adoption Assistance – An employee can exclude a maximum of $13,570 (2017) for qualified adoption expenses paid or reimbursed by an employer. The exclusion is phased out for higher-income taxpayers.	Retained – The House Bill would have repealed the exclusion, but the conference agreement retains the exclusion in its current form.
Tax Rates	
There are seven tax brackets: 10, 15, 25, 28, 33, 35 and 39.6%.	There will continue to be seven tax brackets but at different rates and thresholds. The rates are: 10, 12, 22, 24, 32, 35 and 37%
Child Tax Credit	
Allows a credit of $1,000 per qualified child under the age of 17. The credit is reduced by $50 for each $1,000 the taxpayer's modified gross income exceeds $75K for single taxpayers, $110K for married taxpayers filing joint and $55K for married taxpayers filing separate. Taxpayers are eligible for a refundable credit equal to 15% of earned income in excess of $3,000. There is also a special refundable computation when there are 3 or more qualifying children.	Retains the "under age 17" requirement and increases the child tax credit to $2,000, with up to $1,400 being refundable per qualified child. The credit phases out for taxpayers with AGI over $200,000 ($400,000 if married joint). Thresholds are not inflation-indexed. Child must have a valid Social Security Number that is issued before the due date of the return to qualify for this credit.

Non-child Dependent Credit	
No prior credit. New for 2018	Allows a $500 non-refundable credit for non-child dependents. Same phaseout rule as for Child Tax Credit.
Alternative Minimum Tax (AMT)	
Individuals – 2017 Exemption amounts are $84,500 for married taxpayers filing jointly, $42,250 for married filing separate, and $54,300 for single and head of household. The exemption phase-out thresholds are: $160,900 for married taxpayers filing jointly, $80,450 for married filing separate, and $120,700 for single and head of household.	Retained, but the exemption amounts are increased to: $109,400 for married taxpayers filing jointly, $54,700 for married filing separate, and $70,300 for single and head of household. The exemption phase-out thresholds are increased to: $1 Million for married taxpayers filing jointly and $500K for others.
Corporate	Repealed
Education Provisions	
American Opportunity Credit (AOTC) –The AOTC provides a post-secondary education tax credit of up to $2,500 per year, per student for up to four years. 40% of the credit is refundable. The credit has a phase-out threshold of $160K for MFJ filers (no credit allowed for MFS) and $80K for others.	Retained - The House Bill would have extended the credit to a fifth year, but the conference agreement retained the credit in its current form.

Lifetime Learning Credit (LLC) –LLC provides annual credit of up to $2,000 per family for post-secondary education. The credit has a phase-out threshold of $112K for MFJ filers (no credit allowed for MFS) and $56K for others.	Retained - The House Bill would have repealed the LLC, but the conference agreement retains the credit in its current form.
Sec 529 Plans – These accounts allow non-deductible contribution and provide for tax-free accumulation if distributions are used for post-secondary education expenses.	Amended to allow tax-free distributions of up to $10K per year for grammar and high school education tuition and expenses.
Discharge of Student Loan Indebtedness – Excludes from income the discharge of debt where the discharge was contingent on the student working a specific period of time in certain professions and for certain employers.	Modified to exclude income from the discharge of indebtedness due to death or permanent disability of the student.
Higher Education Interest – Allows an interest deduction of up to $2,500 for interest paid on post-secondary education loans.	Retained - The House Bill would have repealed the higher education interest deduction, but the conference agreement retains the deduction in its current form.
Tuition Deduction – Allows an above-the-line deduction for tuition and related expenses in years before 2017. The amount of the deduction is limited by AGI and the maximum deduction for any year is $4,000.	Retained - The House Bill would have repealed the tuition deduction, but the conference agreement retains the deduction in its current form. This means that the termination date of December 31, 2016 still applies, so this deduction would not be allowed for 2017 and later.

Employer Provided Education Assistance – An employer is permitted to provide tax-free employee fringe benefits up to $5,250 per year for an employee's education.	Retained - The House Bill would have repealed employer provided education assistance, but the conference agreement retains the assistance in its current form.
Exclusion of Qualified Tuition Reduction – Employees of educational institutions, their spouses and dependents may receive a nontaxable benefit of reduced tuition.	Retained - The House Bill would have repealed the exclusion from income of tuition reductions, but the conference agreement retains the benefit in its current form.
Home Sale Exclusion	
Generally, where a taxpayer owns and uses a home as his principal residence for 2 out of the 5 years prior to its sale, the taxpayer can exclude up to $250,000 ($500,000 for a married couple) of profit from the sale.	Both the Senate and House bills would have changed the qualifying period to 5 out of 8 years, and the House bill would have phased the exclusion out for higher income taxpayers. The conference agreement retains the current law.
Estate & Gift Taxes	
$5.49 Million (2017) is exempt from gift and/or estate tax. This is in addition to the annual gift tax exclusion, which for 2017 is $14,000 per gift recipient.	The exclusion is increased to $10 Million adjusted for inflation since 2011, which is estimated to be approximately $11.2 Million. The annual gift tax exclusion is retained. The House Bill would have repealed the estate tax for decedents dying in 2025 or later, but the conference agreement did not include this provision.
Entertainment Expenses	

A taxpayer who can establish that entertainment expenses or meals are directly related to (or associated with) the active conduct of its trade or business, generally may deduct 50% of the expense.	No deduction is allowed for (1) an activity generally considered to be entertainment, amusement or recreation, (2) membership dues with respect to any club organized for business, pleasure, recreation or other social purposes, or (3) a facility or portion thereof used in connection with items (1) and (2). Also disallows a deduction for expenses associated with providing any qualified transportation fringe to the taxpayer's employees. Employers may still deduct 50% of the food and beverage expenses associated with operating their trade or business (e.g., meals consumed by employees on work travel).
Tax Credits	
Adoption Credit– Provides a credit of up to $13,570 for child under the age of 18 or a person physically or mentally incapable of self-care.	Retained – the House Bill originally repealed this credit, but the credit is retained in the conference agreement.
Sec 1031 Exchange	
There is non-recognition of gain when taxpayers trade properties of like-kind that are used for business or investment.	For exchanges completed after December 31, 2017, only real property will qualify for Sec 1031 treatment.
Net Operating Loss (NOL) Deduction	

Generally, a NOL may be carried back 2 years and any remaining balance is then carried forward until used up or a maximum of 20 years unless the taxpayer elects to forego the carryback and carry the loss forward only.	The 2-year carryback provision is generally repealed after 2017 except for certain farm losses. Beginning after December 31, 2017, the NOL deduction is limited to 80% of taxable income (determined without regard to the NOL deduction) for losses arising in taxable years beginning after December 31, 2017.
Sec 179 Expensing	
A taxpayer can elect to expense up to $510,000 of tangible business property, off the shelf software and certain qualified real property (generally leasehold improvements). The annual limit is reduced by $1 for every $1 over a $2,030,000 investment limit. The Sec 179 deduction for certain sport utility vehicles is capped at $25,000.	For property placed in service after 2017: The annual expensing and investment threshold limits are increased to $1,000,000 and $2,500,000, respectively, with both subject to inflation indexing. SUV cap to be inflation-adjusted. Definition of Sec 179 property expanded to include certain depreciable tangible personal property – e.g., beds and other furniture, refrigerators, ranges, and other equipment used in the living quarters of a lodging facility such as an apartment house, dormitory, or any other facility (or part of a facility) used predominantly to furnish lodging or in connection with furnishing lodging.

	Expands the definition of qualified real property eligible for Sec 179 expensing to include any of the following improvements to nonresidential real property placed in service after the date such property was first placed in service: roofs; heating, ventilation, and air-conditioning property; fire protection and alarm systems; and security systems.
"Luxury Auto" Depreciation Limit	
Annual limits apply to passenger autos used for business on which depreciation is claimed. For vehicles placed in service in 2017 the limits are $3,160, $5,100, $3,050 and $1,875, respectively, for years 1, 2, 3, and 4 and later. If bonus depreciation is claimed, the first-year limitation is increased by an additional $8,000.	For passenger autos placed in service after 2017 the maximum amount of allowable depreciation is increased to the following amounts if bonus depreciation is not claimed: $10,000 for the placed-in-service year, $16,000 for the 2nd year, $9,600 for the 3rd year, and $5,760 for the 4th and later years. Amounts will be indexed for inflation after 2018.
Excess Business Losses For Individuals	
Losses, other than passive losses, were allowed, and if a net loss was the result, a NOL deduction was created and carried back 2 years and then forward 20 years until used up.	A taxpayer other than a C corporation would not be allowed an "excess business loss." Instead, the loss would be carried forward and treated as part of the taxpayer's net operating loss (NOL) carryforward in subsequent taxable years.

	Excess business loss for a taxable year is defined in the Act as the excess of the taxpayer's aggregate deductions attributable to the taxpayer's trades or businesses for that year, over the sum of the taxpayer's aggregate gross income or gain for the year plus a "threshold amount" of $500,000 for married individuals filing jointly, or $250,000 for other individuals. The provision will apply after taking into account the passive activity loss rules.
ACA Individual Insurance Mandate	
Anyone who does not meet one of the limited exemptions must have health insurance or pay a penalty.	Repealed, effective 2019.

Bibliography

Largest Tax Cut in History? - FactCheck.org. (n.d.). Retrieved 11 24, 2018, from https://www.factcheck.org/2017/11/largest-tax-cut-history/

Tax Benefits for Education: Information Center. (n.d.). Retrieved from IRS.gov: https://www.irs.gov/newsroom/tax-benefits-for-education-information-center

(n.d.). Retrieved from https://doeren.com/tax-reform-individual-amt-corporate-amt/.

https://tax.thomsonreuters.com/news/2017-tax-reform-checkpoint-special-study-on-individual-tax-changes-in-the-tax-cuts-and-jobs-act/. (n.d.). Retrieved from https://tax.thomsonreuters.com/news/2017-tax-reform-checkpoint-special-study-on-individual-tax-changes-in-the-tax-cuts-and-jobs-act/.

Largest Tax Cut in History? - FactCheck.org. (n.d.). Retrieved 11 24, 2018, from https://www.factcheck.org/2017/11/largest-tax-cut-history/

Tax Benefits for Education: Information Center. (n.d.). Retrieved from IRS.gov: https://www.irs.gov/newsroom/tax-benefits-for-education-information-center

Steven Wiebler CPA - Highlights of the Tax Cuts and Jobs Act. (2018). Retrieved from https://www.stevenwieblercpa.com/highlights-of-the-tax-cuts-and-jobs-act/

Summary: Tax Cuts and Jobs Act of 2017 – Paragon Financial Partners. (2018). Retrieved from http://paragonfinancialpartners.com/summary-tax-cuts-and-jobs-act-of-2017/

Investor Bulletin: An Introduction to 529 Plans | Investor.gov. (2018). Retrieved from https://www.investor.gov/additional-resources/news-alerts/alerts-bulletins/investor-bulletin-introduction-529-plans

The Tax Cuts and Jobs Act of 2017 Is Signed into Law - O'Brien Shortle Reynolds & Sabotka, PC. (2018). Retrieved from https://www.vtcpa.com/tax_guide/the-tax-cuts-and-jobs-act-of-2017-is-signed-into-law

Steven Wiebler CPA - Highlights of the Tax Cuts and Jobs Act. (2018). Retrieved from https://www.stevenwieblercpa.com/highlights-of-the-tax-cuts-and-jobs-act/

Tax Cut and Jobs Act Impacts on Claim Settlements - Millennium Settlements Blog. (2018). Retrieved from https://msettlements.com/index.cfm?pg=MLSBlog&blAction=showEntry&blogEntry=6749

Notes

Notes

Printed in the United States
By Bookmasters